Shade No More Pain: Released and Set Free

Tosha R. Dearbone

# SHADE NO MORE PAIN

## RELEASED AND SET FREE

**Compiled By:
Tosha R. Dearbone**

Redemption's Story Publishing, LLC, Houston, Texas (USA)

Shade No More Pain: Released and Set Free

Shade No More Pain
Released and Set Free

Copyright © 2020
Tosha R. Dearbone

All Rights Reserved.
No portion of this publication may be reproduced, stored in an electronic system, or transmitted in any form or by any means (electronic, mechanical, photocopy, recording, or otherwise) without written permission from the author or publisher. Brief quotations may be used in literary reviews.

Print ISBN 13: 978-1-948853-06-4
Digital ISBN 13: 978-1-948853-07-1
Library of Congress Control Number: 2020918125

Scripture references are used with permission via Zondervan at Biblegateway.com. Public Domain

**For information and bulk ordering, contact:**
*Redemption's Story Publishing, LLC*
Angela Edwards, CEO
P.O. Box 62287
Houston, TX 77205
RedeemedByHim@Redemptions-Story.com

Tosha R. Dearbone

# Dedication

*Shade No More Pain:*
*Released and Set Free*
is dedicated to my mother,
**Esther Marie Battle.**

In August 2019, I remember when God directed me to move back home with her because I didn't leave "the right way." At the time, I didn't realize He was sending me back to make things right and to rebuild our broken relationship.

During the process, each day came with its own challenges, but my mother and I began to see that our way of communicating had shifted. We have COVID-19 to thank for our forced time together, but it was worth it. When she asked me to sit with her to do a Bible study on Proverbs, WOW! It was then I had no doubt God was at work in both of our lives.

Today, I am grateful I heard and listened to God's voice. I believe returning to my roots was just what I needed to be **RELEASED AND SET FREE.** Not just me, though; my mom, too. She is now able to be more open about her past and begin her healing process. I give all glory to God.

*~ Tosha R. Dearbone ~*

# Acknowledgments

I want to first give honor and thanks to God for this opportunity to sow into the lives of all who read this amazing piece of literary art.

To each of the women who shared their experiences in *Shade No More Pain: Released and Set Free*, you are beyond words of greatness!

A special thank you to **Latoya Christman** for agreeing to write the Foreword. You are a true jewel in my life, and I thank God for you. I wish you nothing but success in every area of your life.

To **Angela Edwards**, CEO of Redemption's Story Publishing: Thank you for all of your hard work in assembling this project and for working alongside each one of us as we shared our stories. With your dedication and passion behind this collaborative work, we are grateful for your services.

Last but not least, I want to thank my children for being by my side through it all. You saw things in me that I didn't even see in myself. I love all of you and my grandbabies, Trinity and Amir.

Tosha R. Dearbone

# Foreword

In 2001, R&B Singer Mary J. Blige released a song entitled "No More Drama." I remember when I heard the song for the first time and how it brought back so many memories of bad break-ups in high school and many bad mistakes I regretted. The song expressed the pain and hurt that so many women — whether young or old — could relate to.

*"No more pain (no more pain);*
*No one's gonna make me hurt again."*

Those words rang true to my ears as the words came off the pages of *Shade No More Pain*. The stories within exhibit women who were done with the pain and drama from past rejection, disappointment, and mental, physical, verbal, and sexual abuse. Being women who didn't see the value of what God possessed on the inside of them is now a thing of the past!

As I read each story, all I could think was, *"Wow! It really takes a strong, bold, confident, healed, and transparent person to tell such heartfelt stories!"* I could feel the embarrassment, weariness, and feelings of inadequacy that most women have felt at some point in their lives. I commend these ladies for the openness and vulnerability it took to expose the enemy as they took back their identity. They placed their trust in something bigger and stronger, and that is what is important.

In Jeremiah 17:7-8, it states the person who trusts in the Lord, whose confidence, indeed, is the Lord, is **BLESSED**. He [She] will be like a tree planted by water: it sends its roots out toward a stream, it doesn't fear when heat comes, and its foliage remains green. It will not worry in a year of drought or cease producing fruit.

During the most painful moments of these ladies' lives, they trusted in God—not in human strength. Their power to leave toxic situations and to reclaim their identity came from God and Him alone, and, as a result, they were and are **BLESSED!**

*Shade No More Pain* is a book that reveals the true essence of what it's like to live your life in a mental hospital, hoping the doctors will find a cure. It's filled with hope, self-awareness, and newfound love in oneself. It must be noted this book is not for the faint-hearted, the judgmental person, or the person who condemns or throws "shade." Rather, it is for those who are looking for answers or feel defeated, lost, hopeless, and just tired of feeling trapped.

Tosha R. Dearbone

As a Christian and leader in the community, I am aware of the stigma attached to telling stories such as these. Sadly, they are looked at as "wrong" and "embarrassing." As women, we are expected to keep up a façade by always looking a certain way, acting a certain way, and conducting ourselves in a certain way when faced with abuse. We're even told things such as, *"What goes on in the home – whether good or bad – should stay there."* That is the **wrong** way of thinking.

Sexual, verbal, and physical abuses are happening in the homes of many believers…*and they are silent.*

I decree and declare this very day that as you read these stories, they will give you hope and encourage you to speak up and speak out. You, too, can be delivered, healed, and made whole—just like these women. Forgive yourself. Forgive those who hurt you. Forgive those who betrayed you. Then, begin to **LIVE**! It's not easy, but telling your story gives others hope that forgiveness can happen with the help of the Lord.

I thank Tosha Dearbone for taking on this mantle. It is not easy trying to fulfill what God has called you to be. Tosha, you are an angel and friend that so many people wish they had in their lives to help and encourage women to tell their stories. The gift to help others is rare, and God knows it's not easy.

Shade No More Pain: Released and Set Free

Thank you, Tosha, for giving these women a platform on which to share their stories and for allowing me to be a part of such an incredible journey. To whom much is given, much is required. You, my friend, have shown what is required.

To the readers, I pray this book will find you in a place of expectancy and that you are truly blessed, just as I was.

God Bless!!!

*~ Minister Latoya Christman ~*

# Table of Contents

| | |
|---|---|
| **DEDICATION** | VI |
| **ACKNOWLEDGMENTS** | VII |
| **FOREWORD** | VIII |
| **ARTHENIUS JACKSON** | 1 |
| 20 Years of Hidden Pain | 1 |
| **DESIRAE JEFFERSON** | 12 |
| Broken Ties | 12 |
| **FRANCESCA THOMAS** | 22 |
| Quiet as It's Kept | 22 |
| **JOHNETTA BENNETT** | 29 |
| The Rose That Grew from Concrete | 29 |
| **KEINOSHA KEATON** | 39 |
| The PAIN from ABANDONMENT and REJECTION | 39 |
| **LATOYA SPANN** | 50 |
| I Won the Battle | 50 |
| **SHALITA MCKNIGHT** | 59 |
| There is Purpose in Your Pain | 59 |
| **SHERRA BYRD** | 70 |
| Confessions of a DIAMOND: YOU are WORTH IT! | 70 |
| **SHGLENDA GREEN** | 83 |
| Struck Down, But Not Abandoned | 83 |
| **TOSHA DEARBONE** | 91 |
| It Stops Here | 91 |
| **CONCLUSION** | 101 |
| **MEET THE AUTHORS** | 103 |

Shade No More Pain: Released and Set Free

# Arthenius Jackson
## 20 Years of Hidden Pain

When I was six years old, I was introduced to a type of pain in the most pleasurable way. I know that sounds like somewhat of an oxymoron. Allow me a moment to explain why I use those words—**pain** and **pleasure**—interchangeably.

I recall spending the night with one of my older cousins and can vividly remember my uncle pulling me out of bed, taking me into the room next door, and raping me. For those moments, I felt both *pain* and *pleasure*. My six-year-old body and mind had no idea how to process what was happening to me.

The rape started with his fingers stretching and opening my small vagina. In my mind, I heard my screams, yet not a sound fell from my mouth. My eyes watered in response to the immense pain I felt as he ignored the silent cries of my squirming body. When he suddenly shifted positions, what I felt next would change my life forever.

When I returned home, I thought I was still the same little, innocent girl who first walked through my cousin's door. I tried pushing that fateful night to the back of my mind and pretend it never happened. I wanted to live my life as a normal little girl, but it didn't quite go that way. Any time I was in the same room with him, I was reminded of his smell, his touch, and his voice. It made me feel so dirty and disgusting. As a result of the internal torment, I learned how to hide my pain at an early age, and it naturally became a part of who I would become.

I thought my uncle would leave me alone as I got older, but his inappropriate touches and the sexual talk continued. Much like any other *predator*, he knew I was powerless, weak, and vulnerable. When I would visit my cousins, it was nothing for him to call me over next to him when no one was paying attention. He would sneakily touch me and undress me with his eyes. I hated **every** second of it but was too afraid to show it to him or anyone else. Plus, I felt like it was too late to say anything to anyone about that night or even how he continued to touch and talk to me. I believed I would have been blamed for hiding it, so I continued to suffer in silence.

As I became a teenager, he would call the house in the afternoons while everyone was at work, just to "talk" to me. Since there was no caller ID at the time, I could never ignore his calls. His conversations were laden with perversion but would end with him telling me where I could find some money, hidden somewhere just for me — my "hush" money. *(The money would be left outside under a specific brick not too far from the house.)* After some time, I started hanging up immediately after hearing his voice on the other end…and kept taking the money. I felt he owed me that and so much more and told myself I couldn't speak up anyway, especially since I accepted his payment for my silence. **What would my family think of me if I told?** I decided right then that I would forever remain silent.

Roughly eight years ago, I learned how much childhood abuse could affect an individual. I would never have thought my abnormal behavior stemmed from being raped at the age of six and that the assault would affect my life the way that it did.

It may have appeared to everyone around me that I was fine, but I knew inside that something wasn't quite right with me — sexually, mentally, or emotionally. For example, I began masturbating at an incredibly young age. I can remember craving the *feeling* of an orgasm, although I had no idea what it was called. I just knew I had a **hunger** for experiencing that feeling **all** the time. I would sneak into the bathroom during the day to do it or stay awake late into the night. While masturbating, I could hear the perverted whispers of my uncle. Sometimes, I would just break down and cry. Even though I enjoyed the feeling, ugliness, disgust, and embarrassment often overshadowed the pleasure of it all.

As I wore my mask to school, I found myself excelling every year. I was an honor roll student and involved in extracurricular activities throughout my schooling. I may have appeared to be a confident black girl, but I was far from it. I would've never shared with anyone how I felt about myself, but "ugly" would have summed it up. I did not like who I saw when I looked in the mirror. I hated my hair, my body, and felt like I just wasn't pretty enough to be loved. I carried that mentality throughout high school, with my mask covering my painful truth. I believed the guys would never like me, so I didn't even bother trying to date. By the time I reached college, I was so blinded by the media's portrayal of a woman's beauty that I started comparing myself to other women. I wanted to feel beautiful and desired like "they" were.

I tried dating while in college, but that did not work out too well for me due to my horrible communication skills. Over the years, I had learned to bottle up my emotions while building a brick wall that blocked anyone from getting in. I never shared my feelings or emotions; I just hid them. I was genuinely afraid of allowing anyone to hurt me again. So, instead of dating, I decided to use sex to feel better about myself. If guys didn't like me for me, then *maybe* they would have wanted me for what I could do for them.

Meanwhile, all I was doing was hurting myself even more. How I felt about myself continued to worsen with every moment of so-called "pleasure." Being a pastor's daughter didn't help, either. Although I was in service and leading worship every weekend, the hurt, disgust, embarrassment, and feelings of brokenness remained.

I continued to indulge in sexual activities and even questioned my sexuality at one point. At night, depression and suicidal thoughts plagued my mind. There were many nights I fell asleep on a tear-stained pillow. The need to feel beautiful and loved was often overwhelming. I was too afraid to discuss with anyone what I was feeling and going through, but there was one thing that remained constant in my life: my relationship with God.

One evening, in May of 2013, I made the brave decision to break my silence once and for all to my family. Weeks before making that decision, I had meetings with my mentor and told him about everything I was going through—mentally, emotionally, spiritually, and sexually. I had reached a breaking point and was exhausted from feeling so depressed on the inside while hiding behind the mask I wore for everyone else. I was tired of freeing others as I led worship and not being free myself.

## *I was tired of hiding behind the pain.*

That night, as I sat in the living room with my family, the tears would not stop falling. I had written a letter to my mom, telling her everything that happened to me, the effects, and how broken I felt. I also expressed how much I needed and wanted help. When I opened my mouth to speak, and nothing came out, I motioned for my mentor's wife (who was there for support) to read the letter aloud. As she read, I kept my head down because I was ashamed, embarrassed, humiliated, and hurt by each word spoken. When she finished reading, I held my breath and then looked up in anticipation, wondering who would be the first one to speak.

The room was unnervingly silent.

Once the silence was broken, my family embraced me like never before. Receiving warm, tight hugs from those I loved the most was a remarkable feeling. They let me know they would all support my journey and story. They reassured me that I no longer had a reason to feel embarrassed or ashamed because it was not my fault. Several weeks later, I broke my silence among my church family. That time, it seemed even more liberating because I told the story myself.

## Shade No More Pain: Released and Set Free

Months later, after going through counseling and therapy, I took ownership of my story and proudly shared that I was a survivor in group therapy. Before I knew it, I had hosted my first event to raise awareness of childhood sexual abuse at the local university where I was employed.

Each time I shared my story, I could feel the pain, embarrassment, shame, and humiliation being released from my spirit. Giving voice to the pains of my past truly brought on freedom. Although I still experienced some dark times during my healing journey, I felt God beginning to work on the inside of me. I sensed that something extraordinary was destined to come out of my past. I was about to give birth to a passion I never knew could exist from pain. After attending several therapy and counseling sessions, I knew there was more I needed to do. Therapy and counseling were not the ends of the road for me.

In December 2013, I nervously mailed some paperwork for what would become my first nonprofit organization for the upcoming year. "One Touch Transformation" was birthed in January 2014, with a mission to raise awareness of sexual abuse while empowering other victims and survivors. I was very strategic in choosing the name of the organization. Sexual abuse is a taboo topic, and I knew it wouldn't necessarily be one of those groups that quickly rose to the top of everyone's list. I was aware that people would think it was too sensitive of a subject, but that didn't bother me at all. I knew I had to do whatever it took to get the message out there. I chose to include the word "touch" because, for me, that is how it all began. The organization is a product of my life story and something I **definitely** needed as a young girl.

*That one touch* did transform my life, but ultimately, it transformed me for the better.

*That one touch* dragged me through the mucks of pain for many years, but I endured and turned that pain into passion. My passion for healing shows other victims that they, too, can do more than just survive; they can **THRIVE!**

I also committed to pouring back into my local rape crisis center by volunteering my time. I attended their Sexual Assault Awareness events, shared my story, and empowered others by demonstrating what healing looks like as a survivor. If I wasn't speaking, I was singing. I wanted to offer whatever I could because the wonderful group of people that worked at the center at the time had been amazing to me since I first set foot through their doors.

From 2014 to this very moment, "One Touch Transformation" has allowed me to assist several women and men in recognizing they are not alone and that their past does not have to determine their destination. I have enjoyed sharing my testimony of healing, even as it continues to provide healing for myself. I was also inspired to write a song about my transformation. It's titled *Butterfly* and can be found on all digital markets. Through my nonprofit, we have a mentoring program for young girls called "The Butterfly Effect," which enables us to have open and candid conversations about sexual abuse, boundaries, and consent.

I have learned so much about God and myself throughout this entire healing journey, to include knowing that healing is a process and cannot be rushed. It takes both prayer and patience.

Throughout your own healing journey, you may become exhausted and begin to question God by asking, *"When will my healing come? When will this all be over? When will I receive my breakthrough?"* I asked those **same** questions. The best answer I have for you is that when it's your time, **it's your time**. You cannot put a specific timeframe on your healing journey. Honestly, it is an ongoing learning experience that will continue to strengthen you along the way. **Don't give up!**

For those who have experienced a pain *anything* like mine, I earnestly encourage you to uncover the pain, release your story, and finally be **FREE!**

## Reflection Question:

What is it that's stopping you from taking that first step in your healing journey?

Tosha R. Dearbone

# Desirae Jefferson
## Broken Ties

As far back as I can remember, I never felt loved. My childhood was dark, filled with mental trauma and physical abuse I endured since the age of five well into my teen years. The things I was exposed to and accepted as a young girl sealed my fate. Self-destruction took a toll on my life for years. Yet, here I am today as an overcomer and survivor of mental and physical abuse.

*My story begins…*

I recall standing in the corner for hours at a time, instructed by him to stand in a military stance with my hands at my side, nose in the corner. *"You better not say a peep!"* he would bark. I cried the entire time. Often, my mother would be lying right there in the same room. *"Shut up, b\*\*\*h"* or *"Shut the f\*\*k up,"* she would grunt. My only reprieve was when I went to the bathroom. It felt good to sit after having stood for so long in that corner. Eventually, the day turned into night, and I was commanded to go to bed.

I often wondered why my mother forced me to call that man 'dad.' He was **not** my father, so being told to address him as such was something I despised. Instead, I chose to never address him at all so that I would not have to call him *anything*.

The physical abuse he dished out was nothing short of torture and without a cause. He beat me mercilessly with a wooden brush daily and often burned my hands, leaving them red and raw. He felt no guilt, all while my mom looked at me with what seemed like contempt and hatred — which was odd because she was the one who taught me how to run across the street to call the police on him when she told me to! *I used to run so fast to that payphone…* Making those calls was an almost daily occurrence. A few times, he caught me and would drag me back across the street by my hair. I would cry and fight for my life to get out of his grip because I knew there was an awful beating to come, with no one to save me.

I recall telling my mom that he knocked me out a few times. She never seemed to care, for he had knocked her out a few times, too! *We **all** were terrified of that man…*

Desperation and starvation were my "normal." I was even deprived of the necessities that any young woman needed. For example, we lived without hot water in our home for years. We had to boil big pots of cold water to bathe. We never had heat, either. Most times, we were warmed by the oven (when the bill was not paid, we would just freeze). The only other alternative I had was to tightly wrap myself up in the covers on my bed to keep warm.

I heard my mom's cries when he would beat her (years later, that cycle would continue with me). I hated him for abusing her. It seemed my mom's black eye was her "normal." ***"Why doesn't she just leave him?"*** I often wondered. I prayed he would end up in jail or just die. I cannot forget to mention the beatings with the extension cord that were excruciatingly painful. His abusive ways were endless, severe, and tortuous. It was as if he owned us…as if he had a right to treat us that way. **All** day, **every** day, we were subjected to mental and physical abuse.

My mom's forms of abuse were mental and neglect. She would often tell me to lie for her, and if I didn't obey, she would slap me and call me all types of b*****s. I could feel her hatred for me, never understanding why. Yes, she was unhappy. Yes, we were destitute. However, it was not until she met that man—that terrible human being—that our world was turned upside down. He was indeed a son of a b***h! **For ten years**, he beat the mess out of all of us—my mother, brother, and me. **For ten years**, my mother had no voice to defend my brother and me.

Hearing the cries of my mother all those years took its toll on me as I grew up in the impoverished streets of Boston. It took a lot of self-determination to get out. I vowed never to be like her. She looked so beatdown and hopeless. Getting brutally beaten in the presence of her children had to be a horrific experience for her. I often wondered if she ever felt loved.

Mommy, I do not hate you. I found myself with the same kind of man who treated me even worse, so I know your pain. I used to despise you, but now, I forgive you.

*Moving forward…*

As I grew into my teen years and had a child of my own, I learned that my hunger was much greater than my fear of stealing. I stole milk, diapers, and all kinds of food. I remember my mom not allowing me to keep the baby's milk in the refrigerator. *"The back hall is fine enough,"* she would say. It was in the winter, so that's what I did to keep it cool. I tried telling her storing the milk that way wasn't good and that it needed to be refrigerated, but she didn't want me to have any access to the food in there. Soon enough, she put a chain and lock around the refrigerator. She also locked all the cabinets and boarded up her room, all while hoarding food from us. I was heartbroken. I repeatedly stole for her kids, my baby, and me. As often as she could, however, she made me feel so bad.

After over a decade of torture, she finally left the abusive man and met someone new. He didn't really care for me, nor did I care for him. He was awfully mean and strict. My mom would still secretly mistreat my daughter and me, mostly by depriving us of food. **Why did she hate us?**

Time after time, she tried to kick me out of our home. I recall one frigid day when I came home, and the contents of my room were thrown out. My room was bare. No bed. No crib. Nothing. I left soon after that. With nowhere else to go, my baby and I took a cab to a crackhead's house that he rented out. When we arrived, I did as I usually do: I told the driver the money was in the house, grabbed my daughter, and **RAN**—with no intention of paying because I had **NO** money.

My plan was **NO** plan. I was a young woman with no one except my child…and we were starving. As soon and as often as I could, I would steal food and diapers. I would get caught every now and then. I never went to jail but did have to live with the humiliation of handing over the bag of stolen goods. That struggle for survival went on for months. Life was so unfair! I wasn't on drugs, but my behavior was very "feenish." By any means necessary, I had to survive.

My only concern was keeping my daughter safe. I needed to find somewhere we could call "home," so we made the long journey to her paternal grandparents' house. I felt like the worst person in the world as I took each step. Then, when we finally made it, no one was home! I broke down in tears. I was tempted to leave her on the doorstep with a note that read:

**"SHE NEEDS A GOOD HOME, AND SHE IS HUNGRY."**

I didn't do that, though. My brother's girlfriend lived close by, so I left my daughter with her that night. I didn't want to have to drag my baby around in the cold weather with me. When I returned the following day, she was gone. I went ballistic!

*"My daughter! Where is she?!"* I screamed.

*"Your aunt took her,"* came the reply. *"She said she was going to call you."*

I was so confused and blamed my brother's girlfriend for the mess I had caused. You see, my aunt had been trying to gain custody of my daughter for months. When she was called to pick up my daughter, she was then let in on my little secret that I was homeless. Plus, the girl I left my baby with was only 16 years old, which is underage in the court's eyes.

*Enter the Department of Social Services…*

Who knew my decision that night would be irreversible? Who knew I would never hold, hug, and kiss my baby girl again? Who knew I would never pray with her again or simply assure her, *"I will see you again soon"*?

As life would have it, my aunt and the courts refused to give me back my daughter. It has been 30 years, and the pain has never subsided. I still mourn and long for my baby girl. The woman who snatched up my child knew I was young and homeless, so she won. She never let me see my baby, either. As the years progressed, I learned my daughter thought that woman was her biological mother because she told people she gave birth to her. **How sick is that?!** I recall seeing my daughter at a funeral once, and she wanted nothing to do with me. The pain of that day, I will never get over.

So, there I was…all alone with an abusive boyfriend—a relationship forced by my mother. The few times he beat me were horrible. I felt lost and in pain. My brother used to call me often during that time, but then he stopped. I was concerned for him because he, too, was homeless and couldn't come to where I laid my head because of ill feelings between him and the guy I lived with. I was depressed and confused. I missed my brother and called everywhere trying to find him but couldn't.

One night while watching the news, I got an eerie feeling. When I called my mother's house, I found out her number was changed. (Wow!) I then called her job, was told she wasn't there, and was asked, *"Do you know what happened?"*

*"No. I have no number for her. She moved and changed her number. I only know her work number."* The person on the other end of the line told me the awful news: my brother was murdered. *"I didn't know."*

*"You should call your mom,"* they instructed.

I dropped the phone. I was **devastated**. I had no one else to call, no one to comfort me. I then called the operator and asked them to make an emergency call. They located my mom for me, and when we talked, she told me to come right away and that she needed and loved me.

I couldn't figure out how to get to my mom but needed to make a plan. At that moment, the guy I roomed with came home. I was so distraught and crying…and he was so coldhearted. He hit me, dragged me into the hallway, and banged my head against the wall. **I WAS SO SHOCKED!** I almost *died* that day. Somehow, I got away from him and made it to my mom (I honestly do not recall precisely how because at some point, I blacked out).

*My story doesn't end there…*

My family believes I am to blame for my brother's death. They have shunned me and said they **knew** I was there. Although I am **NOT** to blame…although **NO ONE** believes me, I maintain my strong will to get the *TRUTH*. My mom tells everyone but me that I am the one to blame. **I did *NOT* kill my brother!** Hell, if I were there, it would have been a double homicide! I would lay down my life for that kid…my bro…my best friend.

I have never genuinely laughed since that day. My brother's death stole my innocence and left me empty.

## Reflection Question:

If you had a family member or friend who felt lost and hopeless, what would you say or do to encourage them?

_____
_____
_____
_____
_____
_____
_____
_____
_____
_____
_____
_____
_____
_____
_____
_____
_____
_____
_____
_____

# Francesca Thomas
## Quiet as It's Kept

*"Be a mother who is committed to loving her children into standing on higher ground than the environment surrounding them. Mothers are endowed with a love that is unlike any other love on the face of the earth."*

*~ MP Hinckley ~*

*https://www.azquotes.com/quote/1496717*

~~~~~~~~~~~

That is a beautifully-stated quote; however, it is not the storyline of my life. The memories of my mother do not sound as poetic.

My mother gave birth to me at the age of 23, left her family, and began living an estranged life with my father — a man who was living a life of crime. His crimes led to both my parents being incarcerated when I was a toddler. Strangers left me on the doorstep of family members where I was found and cared for. Upon my parents' release, we were moved to a new state, which only meant "same patterns, different jail cells." When my sibling came along, he and I clung to each other for security and safety.

Eventually, our little family settled into another new home in another new state. Life behind those walls became even scarier, as I witnessed instances of domestic violence. As a result, my mom would leave for prolonged periods, leaving my brother and me to make our own way. I became familiar with the neighbor — an older woman who had a male residing with her — and would go over to visit. While there, the man molested me and instructed me not to tell anyone about our "playdate." Those playdates came to an abrupt end when, at 3:00 a.m. one morning, I awoke and told my dad about the pain I was having in my vagina.

I cannot recall where my mother was at that time. Neither can I remember how long it took for her to make her way back into our lives. I do, however, know that her absence contributed to the pain I was mentally experiencing that went beyond the point of her return. The wound never healed and, therefore, a mother-daughter bond never blossomed.

As life continued, I began to see less of my dad and more of the men my mother brought into our home — a home that was infiltrated with perverted minds that would eventually lead to perverted actions against my frail body and innocent mind. Still, I kept quiet and was cast into another pit of hell. There was an older man who lived upstairs and needed help tending to his household chores. I was permitted to assist him…unsupervised. While there, he would have his way with my premature body, fondling me to fulfill his perverse needs. Out of guilt, he would then take me shopping and buy things for my siblings and me—a gesture that kept my mom sending me back to him.

During that time, my mom was introduced to crack cocaine, causing her to neglect her parental responsibilities. I suppose it was all the more reason for her to "lend me off" to the man upstairs. Around that same time, her new boyfriend was introduced into our lives, and he was a drunkard. He often came home early in the morning, come to my bedroom window, and call out for me to open the door to let him in. I would do as he said and, before I could return to my room, he would lure me to the couch and try to penetrate me. My loud moans and uncontrollable cries were the only things that stopped him.

Still, I remained quiet about the molestation while on the inside, I was crying out for it all to stop.

My mom's drug abuse grew progressively worse, causing her extended stays in the Harris County Jail. Meanwhile, my siblings and I transitioned into the home of a family friend. While there, it wasn't too long before the numbing feelings made their way into my soul again when a male resident began his sexual assaults against me. Night after night, as everyone else slept peacefully, I laid in my bed, pretending to be asleep. I hoped and prayed he would lay elsewhere, but it was not to be. His disgusting touch made its way into the depths of my being. Fortunately, his time with us did not last long. The day he left, I internally celebrated his exit.

When my mom came home from one of her stints in jail, she moved us into our own place. Sadly, because she was still an addict, I became the caretaker, ensuring my siblings had food, made it to school, etc. After school, we would visit a family friend and, one evening, I set out on a mission to buy one of my favorite treats: a pecan log. On the way, I caught the attention of a guy from the neighborhood, and the next horror movie began production. I was dragged off my bike across the street from his home and into his bed of hell. I wrestled. I screamed. I cried. It was all to no avail. When he penetrated my virgin walls, I screamed for my very life. It was then I heard a voice calling his name from a distance, asking him, *"What's that noise?"* He hurriedly pulled himself off my frail body. I ran out of the room and past the distant voice that stood at his door. I made my exit and ran back across the street into the neighbors' yard, trembling with fear. They drew their own conclusions from hearing my screams and seeing the blood running down my legs.

The police and my mom were contacted. In exchange for drugs, my mom agreed to drop the charges. However, considering I was a minor, coupled with the seriousness of the circumstances regarding the incident, the state picked up the case.

Can you begin to imagine what life was like for me in the neighborhood once the cat was out of the bag?

I had to relocate due to threats on my life, shaming, people telling me it was all my fault, and other accusatory words. I was gone for about a year or so, which we thought would be enough time to let things die down and forget about me and what happened. We could not have been more wrong. My mom was still on drugs and regularly "visited" her jail mates. As well, we were living in a shelter.

I remember perfectly the morning of the first day of the trial against my rapist. The prosecutor came to pick me up from the shelter to take me to the courthouse. *(Did you catch that? I said **ME**!)* I recall it being cold as I sat alone in the hallway until

I was called to the stand. I had not seen my assailant since the day he stripped away my innocence. That didn't stop the courts from doing their job of asking me to identify him. At that moment, I froze, and the room fell silent.

"Physically frozen" is a term associated with tonic immobility: a temporary and involuntary paralysis stemming from intense fear. Each sexual encounter I had experienced taught me how to escape psychologically. As I reflect on the rape, being physically frozen helped me endure the moment and made the experience seem less like an assault because my body was familiar with the shock.

For years, I remained quiet, hoping to avert unfair social myths and biases that far too often push victims into shadows, leaving them afraid to step forward and seek the help they desperately need. As I think of who I am today — a mother, a survivor, an educator, and a mentor — I realize that piece of my life is meant to present the message that molestation and rape do not have to define you. Yes, they are horrific events, but they are also survivable.

## Reflection Question:

As a mother, why is it important to exhibit behavioral, cognitive, and emotional characteristics that can specifically and directly be associated with the ability to care for and keep a child safe?

_____
_____
_____
_____
_____
_____
_____
_____
_____
_____
_____
_____
_____
_____
_____
_____
_____
_____

Shade No More Pain: Released and Set Free

# Johnetta Bennett
## The Rose That Grew from Concrete

I recall visiting my mother's best friend's house with her and my older brother when I was around six years old. Her best friend had a 14-year-old son. My mother always made me go into his bedroom when she and his mother were talking. When I went into his room, he would be playing his video games or reading a comic book...that was until the day came when those forms of entertainment were not enough to satisfy him.

One day, he asked if I have ever felt a boy's penis. I was six years old! I had no idea what a penis was! The blank stare on my face made him realize I didn't know what he was talking about, so he took it upon himself to pull his penis out of his shorts and show me. Instantly, I became terrified, and my body froze in place. He then leaned over to me, grabbed my tiny hand, placed his penis in it, and instructed me to rub. When I didn't obey, he got mad and threatened to beat me up. Out of fear, I complied. That was the first of many sexual incidents with him.

At that tender, young age, I did not know or understand exactly what I was doing.  Sadly, the encounters continued for a few years. They happened so often, I didn't even realize I wasn't supposed to be enjoying what I felt, as each act became my "new normal." I blocked out the fact that it was wrong and told myself that it was okay.

For whatever reason, the friendship between his mother and mine ended, and we stopped visiting them. I was angry because I actually looked forward to going over there. Even though I knew it was wrong, I found myself enjoying the feelings my body experienced, even at that young age.

As time went on, I made myself act as if the sexual abuse never happened. I grew up thinking the only thing a man wanted from me was sex. There was always a void that I could never fill, and I felt sex was the only way I would feel love. My mother never showed me love, so I didn't know what it really felt like. She and I had no relationship, no communication, nothing...

When I got into junior high, I still searched for something to fill that void and give me the feeling I felt when I was molested because, to me, that was the affection I was missing. I tried talking to multiple boys throughout my years in school, but for whatever reason, they were not interested. I then started talking to older men. At one point, I started dating my friend's older cousin. I was 16 at the time, and he was twenty-six.

I must note here that when I was molested, there was never any penetration, just oral and fondling.

So, I was involved with a 26-year-old man who gave me all of the attention and affection I was missing. The fact that he was in a gang was just amazing to me because he was the first "street dude" I had talked to. Not only did he spoil me, but his lifestyle also excited me. One day, while my mother was at work, I let him come over to my house. When he asked me if I had ever had sex before, I explained I had never been penetrated but had done "other things." I lost my virginity to him that day. After it happened, feelings of loneliness and a deepening void enveloped me, although I continued dating him on and off during my high school years.

As stated, my mother and I never had a mother-daughter relationship. The extent of our communication was when she came home from work, opened my bedroom door, said hello, and then closed the door. My mother was also a minister, so I was in church almost every day throughout high school — yet at the time, I was dating a grown man. For years, I carried the weight and embarrassment of being molested as a child. I felt like everything was my fault. I was hurting on the inside, and the little girl in me silently cried out for help. Still, I could not tell my mother or brother what happened to me, so I numbed the pain by being promiscuous.

When I graduated from high school, I attended the University of Houston Downtown for about a year. When my father passed away, I decided to leave Houston, Texas, and move to Jacksonville, Florida, with my father's side of the family. I was 18 going on 19 when I relocated.

I recall the ease in which I could get into the local nightclub in Jacksonville because one of my family members owned the club. That was when my promiscuity got worse. I started working for Aetna and got my first apartment shortly after at the age of nineteen. Even though I had my own apartment and family nearby, I was still lonely and searching for a way to fill that void. I often called the phone chat lines at night and talked to different guys because it made me feel wanted. The only thing on my mind was filling that sexual void, so I met up with some of those guys and had sex. Emotionally, I had become numb and simply went through the physical motions…trying to fill that void.

Well, I ended up losing both my job and apartment. In 2000, I moved to Atlanta with two of my cousins. I just knew it was a new beginning! I got a good job and didn't mess around with anyone for quite a while.

After about six months or so, I started dating a guy I had only known for two weeks. On Valentine's Day, he invited me to his house. *(At the time, I was a heavy drinker and could finish a whole bottle of vodka by myself because it temporarily numbed the pain I continued to battle.)* His gift to me was a bottle of Absolut vodka and two magnetic kissing bears from Hallmark. I guess because he was so high and drunk, he felt as if I didn't appreciate his gifts and got very upset. He wanted a kiss; I didn't. He wanted to have sex; I didn't. When I told him no, he grew enraged, pulled out a gun, and made me strip naked as he held me at gunpoint. He then made a phone call, took my license, and arranged for them to bury me after I was shot and killed.

I heard the voice of the Holy Spirit whisper, *"Call his bluff."* From within my spirit, I whispered back, **"You've got to be kidding me!"** Again, the voice said, *"Call his bluff."*

So, I boldly told him, *"If you were really going to shoot me, you would have done so already."*

He looked at me as if I had lost my mind! That man had a gun to my head, and I was talking smack! ***"Are you crazy?!"*** he yelled.

*"Maybe I am. If you were going to kill me, you would have done it already,"* I replied. *"Let's stop wasting each other's time. Let me call somebody to come to pick me up."*

When he told me to go ahead and make that call, his hands were visibly shaking. He obviously couldn't believe I said what I did. The trauma didn't stop there, though! He had more instructions to dish out:

*"Have whoever picks you up, pull up with no lights on. You walk out to the street to meet them. The whole time, I'm gonna keep the gun pointed at you. If they bring somebody with them or if I think they're going to do something to me, I will shoot you on sight."*

I called one of my cousins, and she came to pick me up…just like he instructed.

After that "situation," I told God, *"You have to change me, Jesus. You must **save** me."* However, I didn't stop doing whatever I felt like doing.

I ended up meeting a man who happened to be from Texas, too. We were in a serious relationship and eventually got engaged. I didn't know he was part of the Atlanta street life because he was in the Air Force. I'll never forget the day that changed my life forever...

I was shopping for furniture and kept calling my fiancé. After repeated tries and getting no answer, I called his father's house. His father said, *"Baby girl, did you not see the news?"*

*"No,"* I replied. Now, mind you, I had just talked to my fiancé earlier. His last words to me were, *"I love you."* Two hours later, he was killed in a drug-related incident.

Again, I cried out to Jesus: ***"Please save me! I'm lost!"***

At that point, I was suicidal and tried to kill myself. It seemed as if everything from my childhood through adulthood had built up, and I didn't know what else to do. After an obviously unsuccessful attempt at killing myself, I prayed, started going to church, and diving deeper into God's Word. I became celibate and tried to live right, which was when I met my daughter's father.

Two years into our relationship, the physical abuse started. I was slapped, kicked, and dragged across the floor by my hair. He manipulated me into believing the abuse was all my fault. When I got pregnant with our daughter, the violence didn't stop. Instead, it got worse. He kicked me in my stomach, and he threw me through a wall. That was the breaking point.

I left him and moved to Tampa Bay, Florida, with my mother. I then started attending Paula White's church. I'll never forget the night Kelly Price was there singing. I had to be about six to seven months pregnant at the time. When Paula and Kelly had an altar call, I went forth and rededicated my life to Christ. I told Jesus from that point on, I would live my life for Him. I immediately felt a change come over me. It was unexplainable! I began to cry so hard, and, as I cried, it felt like the abused little girl in me was finally getting her chance to release her pain and shed the tears that had been held in for so long.

A few weeks after I rededicated my life to Christ, I finally sat down with my mother and told her all that happened to me as a child and how I felt that she nor anyone else really loved me. For the first time in my life, I saw my mother express emotions. It was then she told me that she, too, had been molested as a child and couldn't show me love because her mother never showed her love. After we talked, I decided I would do everything in my power to break the generational curse over my family. I refused to allow those things to happen to my daughter.

Let me say this: Yes, I rededicated my life to Christ, but I am far from perfect. I still make mistakes every day of my life. The difference now is that I no longer beat myself up about them. I work on those "weak areas" and keep moving forward.

You must understand and believe that everything you have gone through and endured is all for a greater purpose! Never feel bad or embarrassed about anything you have dealt with because it was designed to make you the woman you are today and who you are becoming! I want you to know that the **ONLY** person who can fill any void in your life is God. No drug, drink, or man can do it.

**Remember: Like the rose that grew through the concrete, so shall you!**

## Reflection Question:

Thinking back to your childhood, was there ever a time you felt unloved by your family or friends? What have you done since then to realize self-love is essential?

## Keinosha Keaton
## The PAIN from ABANDONMENT and REJECTION

Rejection and abandonment can cause people to become angry, bitter, and hateful. They can also trigger feelings of being stuck and defeated. Regardless of its cause, rejection is painful. The pain level varies from person to person and situation to situation. At some point in our lives, we all experience rejection — sometimes, more than we care to admit.

Let me share with you how my pain from abandonment and rejection came to be...

Ever since I was a little girl, I was molested **repeatedly** (and that is no exaggeration). It was a situation that was well outside of my control. Much like many victims of child sexual assault, I remained silent about it for *YEARS* because I thought, *"Who is going to believe my "dad"* (the deacon of the "family church") *molested me? No one is going to believe me...or will they?"* Personally, I didn't think anyone would.

My "dad" wasn't the first man to molest me; he was the second **AND** the one who continued to do so for *YEARS*. The first molester chose me when I was seven years old. No one knew about him because I never revealed to my family who he was.

As my life would have it, the instances of molestation turned into human/sex trafficking. You might be wondering how **THAT** happened. Well, the molestation almost seamlessly turned into me being coerced and traded for things to have sex with other members of my "dad's" family. I was even taken on trips in and out of town and made to have sex with the preacher of our "family church." The men were slick with how they set it up. They would trade me back and forth, all while keeping their dirty little secret and having me believe that neither knew what the other was doing.

I was a motherless and fatherless child, which is how abandonment entered my life. Get ready for a wild ride! I will do my best not to confuse you.

My "dad" wasn't my biological father. He was, however, the only father I knew from birth. When I was a freshman in high school, one of my brothers (who is a twin) informed me that **his** dad was actually my biological father — information he gained from overhearing a conversation between his mother and father. Strange and complicated, huh? Yes, I know. I heard what my brother said but chose to ignore him, all while storing that surprising and new detail in my long-term memory bank. To add to the confusion, my brothers' father was labeled as my "uncle," and their mom was the ***sister of the man who was labeled as my "dad."*** Yep! I told you. Complicated.

So, there I was…fatherless and *confused*. The man who was supposed to be my father wasn't. He was the man I lived with from elementary past high school, yet he was no relation to me whatsoever! **NO RELATION!** *What?!* I could not prove otherwise, so he remained my "dad" as I knew him to be.

I can recall the look of terror on my mother's face when I asked her if the man who raised me or the twins' father was my dad. (Little did I know, the reason she was terrified was that both my "dad" **AND** biological father had raped her when she was around 15 or 16 years old.) My stepmother was the one who confirmed that my twin brothers and I have the same father (I was 39 years old when that was revealed). As for my mother, she was forced to keep the men's dirty deed a secret and was assured my "dad" would take care of me.

So, there you have it. Not only did I not have a father I could claim, but my mom **couldn't** be a mother to me because she was suffering from her own internal pain, silence, and struggles. I was robbed of my childhood by a perverted man, and my mother was always at work or out of the home shooting pool. As an adult, I now understand she was dealing with her own trauma that no one knew about.

As a result of feeling abandoned, I turned to the streets and other men for security. I was looking for love to fill the void of being unloved by my mother and not having a father. (Since my "dad" molested me for years, he was nowhere near what a **father** should have been.)

I have two sisters who were birthed by my mother. They lived with her, so they received more attention than I did. Although I saw my mom every day, when she looked at me, it was as if she were looking at a monster. Often, she would fuss and curse at me to the third degree. That hurt me so bad. As time progressed, my heart grew even darker and hardened by it all. I would talk back to her from time to time and, later in life, cursed at her. I often wondered, *"Why does she speak to me in such a horrible way?!"* I was treated more like someone off the street rather than her daughter.

She had **no idea** what I was dealing with. I was in a dark place and needed my *mother* but could **never** tell her what was happening to me.

Favoritism was shown towards my sisters. Although my mother was there when I gave birth to my children (she was the one who drove me to most of my doctor's appointments and the hospital), she did not do much for them. She did more for my sisters' children, which I am sure is because they didn't have their father in their lives...*like everyone thought mine was.*

I recall how proud my mother was when I gave birth to my son. You see, she always wanted to have three boys, born six years apart. However, God gave her three **girls**—six years apart. Still, my son's birth did not ease the bitterness we held towards each other.

When I was in school, I was rejected. Most people did not want to be my friend. That became noticeable when I was in the fifth grade. I fought hard to be liked and found myself becoming a people pleaser. I wanted to be heard, but no one heard me. My peers used to tease me due to the way I smelled. They didn't know they were smelling the residue of my attacker. As well, I didn't have the things I needed to get and stay clean because of who was raising me. **Who did I have to teach me life skills?** *No one.* Everyone ***assumed*** I knew how to care and fend for myself...but I didn't know! I soon became an outcast—something that would become my norm for many years to follow.

Now, I am sure it wasn't just "dad's" residue that turned others away. It was also because I was wired differently from them. Due to my circumstances, I was a bit more mature than the average child my age. Psychologically, however, I was destroyed. At school, I was counted out. No friends. No mother. No father. Yes, my mother was there physically, but she was emotionally unavailable for me. I was always on my own.

*Abandonment and rejection will cause you to create a mental prison. You become at war with yourself and all the people who abandoned and rejected you. Hatred builds every time they are in your presence.*

As for me, my mind was flooded with negative thoughts. At times, I thought of harming the men who attacked me. When I asked myself the questions, *"Is he my father or not? Why would he do this to me if he is my **father**?"* the reply came back, *"**Fathers don't hurt their children.**"* Oh, but yes, some do. Some abandon and reject their children without realizing it because they, too, have been abandoned and rejected. That doesn't make it right, though. Being on the receiving end is painful and wrong on so many levels. A dysfunctional family with dysfunctional cycles will continue to be one until someone steps up to both **disrupt** and **destroy** those cycles. Who wants to live their life mentally "dead" because of the negative patterns perpetrated by their "loved ones"? **I sure don't!**

I likened being rejected to being sentenced to death, and I was "serving time" because of my biological father's wrongs. Ironically, I am his twin (outside of the fact that I have hair and am a female). My mother rejected me because of her pain and tragedy. She couldn't face her own pain, so she took it out on me. To her, I was a constant reminder of my father and how I was conceived.

Their pain — both inflicted and felt — became a part of my identity. There was no foundation on which to build from the start because it seemed as if everyone in my life was operating in a state of brokenness in some way.

The relationship with my mother wasn't good until the last five years of her life. The last two years of it, she would call and text me often. Three weeks before her passing and before I left Texas for good, she said the following words to me that I will never forget:

*"Raise your children. I am proud of you.*
*Don't ever come back here."*

That meant the world to me. I felt like she **knew** about all that my "dad" had done to me, but she didn't. For far too long, I was not afforded the opportunity to truly bond with her because she was "emotionally removed" from my life. I never had a relationship with my biological father ("uncle"), either.

Unfortunately, he died in 2009. Even as my uncle, I didn't get to know him well. I would see him here and there but never got close to getting to *know* him. All I knew was that he was the twins' father and was married to "my aunt." Plus, he was always at work.

All my **relationSHIPS** didn't last long because I would want to be alone or just stay away and keep people at arm's length. My **relationSHIPS** with people didn't go far because I was afraid of being abandoned and rejected again. *If my own family did those things to me, who's to say a stranger wouldn't?* My **relationSHIPS** with both women and men were unhealthy and toxic because I was always in survival and safety-mode.

*Abandonment and rejection will cause you to fear others and treat yourself with toxicity.*

I finally decided to go to therapy, which was intensive. I had two different therapists and was going to sessions twice a week. I learned I had to heal different stages of my inner child before I could work on my teen and adult years. I had to make the conscious decision that I **wanted** to be healed. It was vital to my life and certainly did not matter how folks viewed me. I was *tired* of feeling as if no one cared. I was *tired* of being invisible. I was *tired* of being rejected. I was *tired* of suffering from trauma. All along, I thought I was undeserving of the good life everyone else had.

As it relates to my relationships with my sisters, to a certain degree, they were strange. I felt like one of them disowned me because I *looked* different from her. As we got older and she started dating (teenage years that turned into marriage), I surely felt abandoned and rejected then. **Whew!** It was almost like I didn't exist at all in her world. When she would call her boyfriend's family members "sis," "uncle," and so forth, I felt horrible because she purposely chose not to recognize me as her sister. Before our mother passed, I moved away. I remember calling home or texting my sisters daily, and them choosing when they wanted to pick up the phone or text me back. Even after our mother's passing, I continued to reach out to them because of the love I have in my heart for them as their big sister. However, three years ago, I slacked off and started contacting them once a month. Nothing changed. They would pick up the phone and say, *"Keinosha, I'm going to call you right back."* They **rarely** did. I used to get so angry and just go to God in prayer. I still did my part but refused to put a lot of energy into maintaining our relationships like I did before.

*Being abandoned and rejected is the worst feeling ever.*

## Tosha R. Dearbone

To you who reads this: Know that you matter. Remember that other people are hurting and suffering in silence just like you. Those things must be addressed so that healing and understanding can begin to take place.

You are worthy of all that you desire!

You are incredible!

You are loved!

You are the best!

I wish you all the healing possible on this side of Heaven!

**Reflection Question:**

What do you believe was the primary dysfunction with the author's family, and how would you address the situation if it were you?

_____
_____
_____
_____
_____
_____
_____
_____
_____
_____
_____
_____
_____
_____
_____
_____
_____
_____
_____

Tosha R. Dearbone

# LaToya Spann
## I Won the Battle

At an early age, I knew I was destined for greatness. What I didn't know was all I would go through to get there.

As a child, I was the pretty, little, outspoken, and spoiled girl everyone loved and adored. However, the things God had planned for my life would cause me to question my existence daily. Many times, I wanted to give up, but something deep within wouldn't allow it. It wasn't until a few years ago when I realized why I was always spared.

War started for me at an early age, but I won the battle!

~~~~~~~~~~

I have great memories of my childhood, but I also have others that will never leave me, no matter how hard I try to forget them. I spent most of my Summers in the country with my grandmother and cousins. We played in the yard, went into town with our granny, and attended Vacation Bible School, where we always had fun mingling with the other kids. As my cousins and I got older, we spent less of our vacations together due to our involvement with various other Summer programs.

## Shade No More Pain: Released and Set Free

One particular Summer season, my life changed forever. That was the year the battle began...

I recall the day being atypically hot. I was doing what most ten-year-old children did in the '80s—watching the soap operas (The Young & The Restless, in particular)—when I was sexually abused. It happened so fast, I thought I was in a movie or a character on a television show. I can remember saying "No!" and that "It hurts!" but neither of my cries stopped him. I was left with a bloody sheet to throw away and was told never to tell because if I did, I would lose the people I loved the most.

That was the worst Summer EVER. I was left bruised, broken, and at war with my young life. The sexual assaults lasted for another two and a half years after that dreadful day.

From that Summer until my teen years, I hated everything about myself. I began to believe that I deserved everything that happened to me. As a result of my low self-esteem, I secretly started cutting myself. In my freshman year of high school, I fell into a deep depression that caused me to talk to others rarely. I went from being sociable to barely speaking, unless it was necessary. Even with that abnormal behavior, no one thought to ask me, "What's wrong?" Silence and loneliness were my "Battle Buddies"—neither of which helped with how I felt on the inside as a person.

In 1998, I was very frail and had lost a lot of weight due to battling bulimia. I didn't know at the time that there was a name for the condition. All I knew was after I ate, I would vomit because, in my mind, I wanted to die from starvation. As a teen, I thought I would perish to death because it was evident to me that cutting myself wasn't right. Another time, I was feeling so despondent, I popped ten Tylenol pills (the number ten was significant to me because that was the age my innocence was stolen, along with my voice). After minutes of feeling dizzy, coupled with an intense headache, I threw up the pills. I then sat on my bathroom floor and cried my heart out—not because I just tried to kill myself, but rather because I was unsuccessful at doing so.

Sexual abuse destroyed my life. My self-esteem was null and void. I had no self-confidence and was a very depressed teen—something no one knew because I always smiled and pushed my way through the pain. I often felt I had to fight to survive, yet there were days when I didn't have the fight in me. I never thought I was good enough or that I would become someone great one day. Even though I had amazing role models in my life and people I looked up to, I was so broken and couldn't accept the good that was given to me at the time. Early on in life, I learned to suffer in silence, which followed me into adulthood.

During my college days, I once had what is commonly known as "a wake-up call." At the time, I was sitting in my car between classes, and everything from the first time I was sexually abused began to replay in my head. I tried but couldn't stop it. All I could do was cry like a baby. Once again, I wanted to end it all because I was being reminded that I was nothing and didn't deserve to try to become someone in life.

I got out of my car and walked into oncoming traffic. It was no one BUT GOD who kept me alive that day. I was almost hit by a utility truck, but all I could do at that moment was stand there, crying uncontrollably. A custodian from Valdosta State University walked up to me and began talking to me. I now know God sent her to save me because I truly wanted to die that day. Although I didn't say a word to her, she walked and prayed with me. She also told me about the counselor that was affiliated with the school and suggested I give her a call.

I couldn't understand why God saved me. After all, I still didn't want to fight to win.

For a long time, I lived with so much pain, bitterness, and anger on the inside of me and hid it well from those around me. You would think I would have taken the time to take care of me and my mental health, but that didn't happen until I entered my 30s. I was tired of living just to survive. I wanted to live life out loud but didn't know how.

My turning point on this journey called "LIFE" came one Sunday in 2017 after I had just about enough of living as "less than." I didn't want to live, but I didn't want to die, either.

I got into my car and drove an hour away from my home to a psychiatric hospital where I admitted myself. That was one of the best decisions I've made in my lifetime. I spent a week in the facility, and I'm forever grateful for that choice. While there, I finally found my voice and was able to tell my story without judgment. Instead, I was shown love and given support. I attended every session, eager to learn how I could overcome the obstacles life had thrown at me when I was that ten-year-old, bright, and outspoken little girl.

Right then, I decided I DID want to live. I decided I DID want to fight—not only for my children but for me!

I prayed and asked God to show me why He kept me alive for so long, and His answer came through clear as day. By the time I exited that hospital, my life's purpose had been made known:

I am to use my voice for those who are just like I used to be: without one.

From that day forth, I began to develop self-love, and it has been a well-worth-it journey. I stopped with the self-sabotaging, too. As well, I have developed a familial type of relationship with a therapist.

Another drastic change in my life occurred when I publicly used my voice to speak to others about the sexual trauma I endured as a child. Once I obeyed God and allowed His Spirit to use me, healing took place. It's been over five years now, and my depression has been decreased dramatically. As well, I have not contemplated or attempted suicide since my life turned around for the better.

Allow me a moment to share with you just some of the trauma I've endured:

- Sexually abused as a little girl.
- Forced to have an abortion at the age of 16.
- Had a miscarriage.
- Am a divorced mom of two.
- I have been jobless.
- Was once homeless — with my two children.

I went through all of that and more, but none of it has kept me from my purpose. I was once bruised and broken, but through it all, I am a SURVIVOR! I MADE IT! It's up to me and only me to heal from the trauma and abuse. I am saving and healing that tender, innocent inner-child no one saw at the age of ten.

God kept me because I was created to break the generational curse and cycle of abuse and trauma in my family. I didn't understand it at the young age of ten, but I now know I am on this earth to do some mighty works.

So, as I said in the beginning, the things that happened in my life weren't intended to take me out; they were designed to shape me into the woman I am today. I can share my experiences to help others like myself — those whose innocence and voice were stolen by the enemy of our soul. I also tell those same people that if they allow the Holy Spirit to use them, He will reveal why they went through all they did.

To you, I say the same and add the following: When you allow the Spirit to lead, you will one day be free from the strongholds of sorrow, anger, depression, guilt, shame, and all the other ugly feelings you have.

Affirm the following daily:

- I AM A CONQUEROR.
- I AM LOVED.
- I AM WORTHY
- I AM SAFE.
- I AM UNIQUE.
- I AM NOT MY PAST.
- I AM CONFIDENT.
- I AM PROUD OF MYSELF.
- I AM ENOUGH
- I AM A SURVIVOR
- I SURVIVED IT ALL.
- **I WON THE BATTLE!**

**Reflection Question:**

How have you allowed God to lead and guide you through the hurt and heartache of your past? What would you tell another young lady who endured something similar to your own life story?

_____
_____
_____
_____
_____
_____
_____
_____
_____
_____
_____
_____
_____
_____
_____
_____
_____
_____
_____

# Shalita McKnight
## There is Purpose in Your Pain

**Date:** March 31, 2016

**Time:** 11:26 a.m.

My seat was hard and *very* uncomfortable. Every woman under the sun knows that sitting on concrete is not the place to be. I was anxious and worried at the same time. *"Okay. Let me get myself together,"* I thought. The heavy door opened, and I was thrown a bag of clothes.

*"Hurry up now and get dressed, ladies. I ain't got all day,"* she taunted.

Quickly, I threw on my clothes, all while my anxiety continued to rise, my palms became sweaty, and my heart beat rapidly. My thoughts about what was to come consumed me. I tried my best to keep it together. *"Lord, help me,"* I whispered.

**"Alright, ladies! Line up and follow me this way!"** she yelled. We—eight other ladies and me—followed, walking for roughly five minutes until we reached a set of double doors. *"Alright, ladies. I hope I don't see you all back here no time soon."*

Walking forward, I stepped out and onto the cement pavement of freedom. I had just completed a 240-day prison sentence and was released into what felt like one of the hottest Summers known to man. On the inside, I screamed, *"I am finally free!"* as I looked around to find my ride home. Once in the car, I let out a sigh of relief and said, *"Thank you, Lord!"*

~~~~~~~~~

**TWO HUNDRED AND FORTY DAYS! 240 DAYS!!!** During the length of my prison stay, God had really dealt with me behind those prison walls. I unearthed every avenue of hatred, anger, rejection, abuse, and doubt that fed my hunger to self-sabotage and landed me behind bars.

My then-marriage was failing, and my daughter was left without all that she had: **ME.** *"My God, how did I end up here? What did I do to deserve this life? Who am I to you, God?"* As I sat on my living room floor devastated, confused, and alone, I began to reflect on what it was that had brought and carried me that far. I looked back deep into the darkest depths of the hurt I endured throughout my life…and there it was.

After the trial and sentencing had taken place in 1993, I thought that somehow, my life that seemed to lack purpose would find and love me, but it didn't. My momma loved me and was **always** there to have her baby's back. She was strong, beautiful, and supportive. What about the rest of the family?

Where were they? No one came to my trial or even talked about it with my momma and me. It was just the two of us.

Where was my father? **I'll wait...**

Grandmother? Aunts? Uncles? **I'll wait...**

Where was the rest of my family? Oh. I know where they were—partying it up with the man who molested me! They didn't want to have anything to do with me. I was considered the 'black dog' of the family (at least that was one of my given nicknames). During the sentencing, my family never believed me or supported my truths. As a matter of fact, they completely *ignored* what happened. It wasn't my fault, though. **I was only 12 years old!**

*I will never forget that night...*

I was hanging out with my cousins and uncle. Surely, I felt protected by my uncle, as he had been in my life all my life. *"Come walk with me over here real quick,"* he said. As soon as we turned the corner, I was grabbed by the face, and my mouth was smothered by hands that reeked of cigarettes and mechanic's oil. I was then thrown to the ground, with both my uncle and his friend taking turns having their way with me. I was violently raped and left on the ground—my innocence *ripped* wide open. My polka dot short set was stained and torn into pieces.

I remember rolling onto my side and then up into a kneeling position. Using the side of the brick building to pull myself up, I managed to stand on shaky legs. Blood streamed down my legs and collected on the leaves and debris below. I fell again, unable to bear the stinging and burning that rippled through my violated lady parts.

That night changed my life. ***Did I ever really have one?***

At an earlier age, I inherited emotional abuse, wanting and desiring love and acceptance from others — especially my family. I believed I looked different from the rest of the folk in my family. I was the only dark-skinned one and was called a 'black dog' or 'black gal' my entire childhood. I was often greeted with, *"Hey, Blacky!"* or another insult related to something black. Those words fought me every time, spewing damage and reminding me of all the dark experiences. I felt unworthy, different, and cast out. While it was easy for others to label me as such, it was just as easy for me to believe I was just that: ***dark.***

I was **dark**-skinned. My life was **dark**. My past was **dark**. The rape was horrific and **dark**. The sky was **black** the night I was raped. Both of my rapists were **black** and wore **black** clothing, too.

## Shade No More Pain: Released and Set Free

*Ugh! Why couldn't I be **normal**?* I wished I were light-skinned like my mother, sisters, and cousins. Maybe then, darkness would have gone to live somewhere else. I believed God didn't like me enough to shed one ray of light my way. Besides my momma, I felt as if no one else truly loved me. *I truly miss her…*

At the age of 13, I was dead on the inside—buried and consumed with rejection and low self-esteem. Most days, I desired death. I did not want to see yet **another** dark day. *Were only bad things destined for my life?* The happiness I displayed before others was all an act. **"I am dark, alright,"** I thought to myself. **"Very dark!"** I was tired of fighting and not living, exhausted from making other people happy, just so I could feel loved. Feelings of disgust with being left out, lied on, and mistreated weighed heavily on me. I had spent my entire life riding a rollercoaster of self-inflicted hurt.

I allowed people to connect to and disconnect from me whenever they felt like it. I was violently raped. I constantly second-guessed myself, not knowing my true identity and only wanting to appear desirable in anyone's eyes…except my own. I was always afraid my family didn't want me around, no matter the relation. I didn't know who I was for most of my life.

I had lost myself in other people. Still, I felt the need to be accepted by them all.

When I had enough, I cried out to God like never before. At that moment, something happened — something that had to do with me on the *inside*. Instantly, I felt the relief of weight being lifted from my spirit. I was suddenly flooded with thoughts of every bad situation I had ever faced, blowing my everlasting mind. It was surreal! I couldn't believe I had survived it all! I was then reminded of how I overcame life's most uncertain times. Admittedly, I am sure I lost my mind several times along the way, but God kept me.

I finally saw myself as God saw me: worthy, beautiful, anointed, and perfect in His image. I was forgiven, healed, whole, redeemed, gifted, set apart, and (most importantly) a shining example of a victorious woman.

- I was taken down but not out.
- I had been robbed but not emptied.
- I had been lied on but vindicated.
- I had been ripped but was not dead.
- I had been locked up but released.
- I lost family but gained myself.
- I had been divorced, yet my Boaz came.

- I was addicted to drugs, but now addiction and deliverance are my ministries.
- I cried late at night because I wasn't happy, but I now have joy.
- I felt like I wanted to die, but now I die every day of self to live for God's glory.
- I was filled with self-hate, but now I'm filled with the power of the Holy Spirit.
- I used to talk negatively, but now have the gift of speaking in tongues.
- I used to desire being loved by other people, but now all I desire lies within myself.
- I used to run the streets, but now I'm running for Jesus.
- I used to hide and self-isolate, but now I isolate in my prayer closet.
- I used to fight hard, but now I go hard—fighting demonic spirits.

*I could go on and on…*

2 Corinthians 5:17 tells us, **"Therefore if anyone is in Christ, he is a new creation. Old things have passed away; behold, all things have become new."** Talk about being born again! I feel good!

Furthermore, Ephesians 5:14 tells us, *"For anything that becomes visible is light. Therefore, it says, 'Awake, O sleeper, and arise from the dead, and Christ will shine on you.'"* I have been resurrected! Resurrection power has fallen upon me! My spirituality shifted from religion to relationship. To God be the **GLORY**, for He and I have become one!

*Resurrection power is the work of God in our lives that reaches into our present and brings us into a union with Him.*

My purpose is to live my truth, to shine, and to spread the ultimate gift: **LOVE**. Do I ever question why I received the hand I was dealt? Nope! Not anymore! I am thankful and honored to have suffered—to be a living testimony for millions of women who have not yet transitioned. I am encouraged daily to keep walking by faith and not by sight. The enemy tried to kill me, but God spoke to me and said, *"In **Me**, you will have eternal life."*

**To my molesters:** I have spent many days wondering how you managed to go through with what you did to me. How did your evil thoughts consume you so much that you took the *innocence* of a child? I pray for you. I pray for your children. I pray for everyone who ignored the little girl who cried out in the darkness for love and help. May you walk in your truths to help deliver lost souls that obtain the spirit of child molestation. May love hunt you down and find you in God's grace and mercy!

**To any woman under the capture of my written words:** You are loved. You are beautiful. You are strong. You are worthy. You are healed. I speak forgiveness over your life. I want to encourage you that you are fearfully and wonderfully made marvelous in God's work. You are an empire of beauty and love. You will not lack *anything* in this season. You are not forgotten. Your nights of crying and feeling empty and undesired are over. Your family no longer has power and authority over your happiness. I command your spirit to be freed by the power of my testimony. I release a fresh anointing and favor over your life. I command the woman of God in you to **RISE** to the peak of your purpose.

As your spirit is being set free, I invite you to join me in declaring: **NO MORE PAIN!** For who the Son sets free is free, indeed! **FLY!**

*Pray the following with me:*

Lord, make me Your vessel. Purge me of anything that is not good. Baptize me with the spirit of forgiveness and acceptance. Lord, I desire to experience Your greatness on levels unimaginable. Teach me how to saturate in Your glory,

God. Forgive those who have hurt me. Show mercy, oh God, for I once hurt. Stand me up straight like a statue, solid in Your Holy Word. God, I beam with Your light as I walk with Your direction. I am no longer a dark child. I am a reflection of You.

*In Your Mighty, Matchless Name, I pray. Amen.*

## Reflection Question:

In those times when you feel unloved, alone, and without a purpose, what is it about your life that causes you to feel that way? How do you overcome?

_____
_____
_____
_____
_____
_____
_____
_____
_____
_____
_____
_____
_____
_____
_____
_____
_____
_____
_____
_____

# Sherra Byrd
## Confessions of a DIAMOND: YOU are WORTH it!

As I begin to write my story and reflect on my childhood, I can see many times when I was being groomed for the likes of a **DIAMOND**. A **DIAMOND** is a transparent and flawless (or almost flawless) piece of stone, especially when cut and polished. A **DIAMOND** is valued as a precious gem.

~~~~~~~~~~

After many years of just merely "existing" — going through life from day to day with no hope for what tomorrow would bring — an awakening happened. No, it was not a huge

"*A-ha!*" moment. It wasn't even an over-the-top, super extraordinary event. Rather, it was a moment of peace, surrender, and solitude…a moment between GOD and me that changed my perspective on my life's journey and the direction in which I was heading. What I then thought was one of life's transitional moments, I now recognize as a part of my development into a beautiful **DIAMOND**.

As far back as I can recall, I was an excellent student and loved going to church. It was the incredible love and peace that encamped about me while there and even after. I was active in our neighborhood library and loved reading. Not knowing it then, but understanding it now, reading allowed me to imagine being in places of the world I could only dream of. Plus, reading kept me productive, and I learned new things.

I was raised by my grandmother—a powerful, strong-willed Christian woman who was also strict and an undeniably no-nonsense parent. "Big Momma" (as we lovingly called her) was tasked with raising her second generation of children: three granddaughters. (My mother was an addict, and my father had simply escaped his responsibility of being a parent.) At any given time, our house was crowded with other aunts and uncles (my grandmother's children) who were also addicts.

Although it seemed negative influences surrounded me, I can honestly say I **NEVER** desired to surrender to anything other than the best life had to offer me. I believe my grandmother's prayers are what carried my sisters and me — and GOD kept us from the snare of the enemy.

Memories of being without my mom at a young age plagued me for years, even after she was clean, sober, and an active part of my life. I recall seeing her walk the streets when she was abusing drugs. I remember seeing her go into a crack house and, when I knocked on the door, was told she was not there. The weird thing was instead of crying about those things, I would pray for her healing.

As for my dad, my youthful memory of him was when I was away from home, and he chose then to tell me he was leaving Houston for good. Oh, the tears I cried! No one knew about my secret desire to be a 'Daddy's Girl,' with him protecting me from the world and his arms there to hold me when I felt scared or alone. Twelve years passed before I saw him again, at which time I introduced him to my then one-year-old daughter.

On October 31, 1996, life as I knew it changed. Big Momma died, leaving behind a legacy of strength, faith, and unwavering love for GOD. It was then that adulthood began for me. I graduated high school in the Spring of '97 and went off to college that Fall. By the Spring of '98, I was pregnant. I dropped out of college, worked a part-time job, and struggled financially. Even during what should have been among the most exciting times of my life, I lived with my mom, *struggled* to work through my pregnancy, *struggled* in the relationship I was in, and *struggled* with my self-worth and self-esteem.

Was that to be my fate? No alcohol or drug addiction, but a life of poverty and discontentment? Was that the way I wanted to raise my daughter? Had the "moment" become my reality? The short answer at the time was **YES!**

For the first year and a half of my daughter's life, I was unemployed. I struggled financially, yet distinctly remember a defining moment that changed my perspective on how I wanted to live and what I was going to do about it...

At the time, I was in the Texas Department for Health and Human Services office (the place where the not-so-fortunate people sign up for food stamps and other support) and was totally disrespected. Basically, the caseworker said I was unmarried, pregnant, and wanted to live off the taxpayers. *"Who is she to judge me?"* I thought. Although I was upset and literally cried the whole bus ride home, her accusatory words moved me to action. *(Needless to say, that was my **LAST** visit to that office!)*

Through many ups, downs, failures, storms, and rough times, each experience was used in my process of transformation.

**NOTE:** You cannot move from one process to the next without a test you must pass to prove you can withstand the pressure of the next level. Being unable to pass the test at any point will cause you to repeat the process. Repeating the process does not necessarily mean failure, though. To build a strong foundation, you sometimes must layer the bricks (in this case, 'lesson') several times to ensure the foundation is invincible. The process equips you to carry out your purpose — **no matter the pressure!**

Once I convinced myself I was ready to move into my purpose, there was one thing that helped me to learn who I was as I accepted me for who **GOD** had destined me to be: confessing those things that were not as though they were. Now, when I started doing that, I didn't truly believe many of the things I repeatedly told myself. However, the more I confessed them, the more I confirmed GOD's truth in my life. I must admit: It took some time and work, but the process by which a "REAL" **DIAMOND** is made always takes longer than cubic zirconia...a mere replica of your authentic self.

## I ask: Are YOU a DIAMOND or a ROCK?

### *Another Memory*

I must have been eight or nine years old at the time. It was a great Sunday morning and, as usual, we were all up getting ready for church. That Sunday, however, was unlike any other. **THAT** Sunday was our Annual Youth Day.

*I remember it clear as day...*

Our youth colors that year were burgundy and pink. The youth had new uniforms, and we were already marching into the church. While all the other children were happily anticipating the moment, I was in tears because I was dressed in my pink Easter suit. Big Momma did not have the money to purchase a uniform for me, so I had to wear what I had (my oldest sister had a uniform someone purchased for her, and my younger sister's Godmother bought hers). I was the 'Lone Ranger,' dressed differently and struggling to march in because of my tears. Big Momma was so mad at me! (I think she was more embarrassed than angry.) Uniform or not, I managed to make it through the program.

The next Sunday, as I came out the door of our home (we lived next door to the church), Sister Doris Jones called me over to her car. As I approached, I saw her pulling out a burgundy and pink uniform dress. She then said to me, *"This is yours, baby!"* Filled with emotion, beaming with excitement, full of joy, and overflowing with love, I began to cry. My feelings from that moment are forever etched in my soul. For a person who only knew me from church to show me that type of extraordinary compassion and love was the best feeling **EVER**! I was not her child, grandchild, niece, or even a distant cousin, yet she saw fit to bless me with that dress. I am sure she saw my happiness and excitement, but what I am sure she didn't know was at that moment, my purpose was revealed. I knew that for the rest of my life, I wanted to be able to give others those same feelings of love and compassion, for no other reason than to bless them. No strings attached.

I would consider Sister Jones a *TRUE* gem…an extraordinary **DIAMOND**. A **DIAMOND** is tough enough to withstand high pressure, but its beauty is gentle and subtle. Sister Jones epitomized strength and beauty while living out her purpose in life! She brought rays of sunshine, even in my seemingly darkest hour.

Some people view "purpose" as a *HUGE* word that proves only to dominate their life, when their purpose is as simple as breathing. It's that thing they do that gives them extraordinary feelings of love and compassion.

**MY PURPOSE** is to give back to those who come behind me, to pour into them the early knowledge I received late, and to give in any capacity where I recognize a void or need.

I decided to live on **PURPOSE**! For many years, I lived in the shadows of others because I was fearful of what others thought and how my actions or decisions would negatively affect my family and friends. That meant I basically put my purpose on hold and lived beneath my calling and destiny to be sure I pleased others. That way of thinking robbed me of years where I could have been living my *GOD-GIVEN* purpose. I allowed fear to paralyze me to the point of self-sabotage. Every time I thought I was ready to act or move in and on purpose, that old "stinking thinking" crept up, and fear would gain a foothold.

In 2010, I was asked to volunteer at a nonprofit organization. As a result of a great work ethic, I was asked to join the Board of Directors. That was a new arena for me. I encountered a lot of new people and many significant goals I had to meet. I literally was so busy that I had no time to sit and think negative thoughts. I worked diligently, raising money to give back to the community in which the nonprofit was located.

In the last months of my tenure, I realized I had accomplished more than I had ever done! Most importantly, I *SUCCESSFULLY* worked, moved, thrived, and lived in my purpose! Fear and self-sabotage had taken a back seat to **COURAGE** and a renewed sense of positive *SELF-WORTH*.

**NOTE:** Many times, when we change our intention (purpose or reason) for doing things, the outcome also changes.

In the past, my objective was "people-pleasing." I made decisions or moves based on others who had no consideration of my life. I chose to make them more important than me, my purpose, and **GOD's** plan for me. The moment I began to live **ON** and **IN** purpose, my life changed. Was it easy? *NO!* What's wrong with wanting more for myself? Nothing!

It was so easy to look at others and want to start where I *THOUGHT* they were in life. (Ohhhh, how many times did I do that?) Looks are deceiving, but mirrors tell the truth. I decided to think about my passions—those things that completely warmed my heart…and then **WENT FOR IT!** I had to leave the "stinking thinking" and the negative words, people, and places behind. I then started to prepare myself with positive thinking, confessions of blessings, prayer, and only those in my circle who were like-minded and wanted to see me succeed. I knew if I took the first steps in faith, **GOD** would help me with the rest.

## *Just for You*

You, my sister, are so awesome! Your beautiful, dark skin is a reflection of Christ Himself. Do not worry about the bullies, teasing, or negative spoken words. God is preparing your mind and heart for what your future holds. You are stronger than you think! The sexual abuse you suffered and never told anyone about... **GOD** is going to heal your heart *AND* deal with the abuser.

Perhaps you have heard very disparaging words from your grandmother, causing you to think she never loved you. Well, she **DID** love you — with all her heart! The only way she knew to strengthen you was to be tough. Often, that meant using language that was inappropriate for a child. The Holy Bible says, *"When thy mother and father forsake us..."* It was not your fault or theirs, although I knew it hurt you tremendously. I know that many days, the pain was unbearable. Allow **GOD** to mend your broken heart. Although your parents were unavailable in your younger years, **GOD** is creating a space in you — a nurturing space for the human treasure He is going to bless you with.

That hole in your heart that is filled with neglect will be replaced with a love so grand, you won't be able to contain it. You will share that immeasurable love with many young girls to help fill the void in their lives as well. The insecurities about your looks, body, and talents will only be a fragment of your imagination. Your transformation is going to be hard but so worth it, as it will change your life forever.

All that you have been through — from having drugs run rampant in your family to the verbal, physical, and sexual abuse to parental neglect — were only tests for your testimony. You will one day soon share with every girl you engage with by your speaking engagements (yes, you are a speaker who will stand on stages and speak your truth), your books (write with the expectation that girls will read them — much like I, Author Sherra Byrd, do), your conferences, and your mentoring. This time in your life may seem difficult, but the secrets you've kept buried deep within will be used to free so many.

Your experiences are set up for a greater you. You are strong, smart, ambitious, beautiful, courageous, and a world influencer and changer. You are a rare jewel, a **DIAMOND** of the highest quality, and (most importantly) are admired and *LOVED!* **YOU** are the apple of **GOD's** eye, and He loves you unconditionally. Your 40-year-old self is amazing and needs you to know this:

**I LOVE YOU SO MUCH! I LOVE YOU! I LOVE YOU! I LOVE YOU!**

**EVERYTHING IS GOING TO BE ALRIGHT.**

Sincerely and Completely Yours,

*Sherra Laniece Simpson Byrd*

## Reflection Question:

How will you honor yourself as the **DIAMOND** that you are?

_____
_____
_____
_____
_____
_____
_____
_____
_____
_____
_____
_____
_____
_____
_____
_____
_____
_____
_____
_____
_____
_____

# Shglenda Green
## Struck Down, But Not Abandoned

*"We are hunted down, but never abandoned by God. We get knocked down, but we are not destroyed."*
**~ 2 Corinthians 4:9 ~**

### *A Life Abandoned*

As a child, I never suspected the things I went through would shape me into the Woman of God I am today. The things I am about to share with you might be familiar. You may be going through something similar as you read this, or you may be trying to find a way out. I pray that the telling of my story will encourage you and that you will see that ALL things truly work together for the good of them that love the LORD—even when you don't know Him for yourself. Everything I endured drew me closer to the One who holds my future in His hands because only He knows the plans that He has for me.

Now, I know to some, what I said may sound crazy. You might be asking, "How in the world can bad be GOOD?" Well, I am about to share what helped me—those things that are factual because they happened to and for me.

~~~~~~~~~~

## Tosha R. Dearbone

Hello. My name is Shglenda Green. I am here to tell you some of my life story and how I was abandoned all my life. In that abandonment, there were so many other seeds that were sown to try to kill me—mind, body, and spirit.

My mother had four children: two girls and two boys. I am the second oldest. I recall that as children, my older brother and I were often left at home alone. We didn't know where our mother and father were, and we would go days and days without food. I remember our grandmother coming over sometimes to bring us food, but when she came, it seemed my mother was always around. For years, all our mom would do was either sleep the day away or never be home—in between having two more kids (we are all close in age).

One day, my siblings and I were home alone with no lights on and no food in the house (we had not eaten for days). Suddenly, there was a knock at the door. When my brother answered it, on the other side stood workers from Child Protective Services (CPS). Someone had called them about our mother's extended absence after she'd been gone for two weeks. The CPS workers removed all four of us from our house and placed us in their car. Fortunately, my grandmother was really close with the neighbors, who called to let her know what was going on. My grandmother arrived just in the nick of time.

When she got there, the CPS workers asked her if she wanted to keep us, and she said she would. So, we ended up living with our grandmother. Had she not come when she did to get us, we would have been placed in the foster care system.

As a six-year-old child, I didn't understand all that was happening to our family. All I knew was that I wanted my mother or father. My family's dynamics were strained:

- My mother was the only child of my maternal grandmother.
- My mother had brothers on her paternal side of the family, but her father wasn't there for her, so I didn't know any of them well at all.
- My father was in and out of our lives, so I had no clue who my uncles and aunts were on his side.

Living with my grandmother and her best friend, whom we called "Auntie," became our permanent living situation. At around the age of 11, I started noticing my grandmother showed more attention to my other siblings.

It must be noted here that my grandmother's sisters and brothers thought it was a bad idea for her to take us in. We would sometimes hear conversations about us to that effect, causing those words to sink into my heart and leaving me feeling unwanted and abandoned.

I recall the time when there was no school, and my grandmother and aunt were at work. As I was asleep, my oldest brother chose to lay in the bed with me and start touching on me. Soon after, we started having sex. Although I was only 11 at the time this happened, the inappropriate touching started early on. The sexual abuse continued for a long time. I even had a cousin who would participate by either watching us or having sex with each other. I was afraid to tell anyone because it seemed like everyone was against me. Plus, I was told not to say anything, or I would get hurt.

Our big brother tormented my younger siblings and me. He would do things to us like make us eat raw eggs and, if we threw them up, he would hit us and make us eat more. I was a bitter and broken young lady. I could not keep friends because I feared being left, rejected, and hurt. I did, however, make friends with a young lady in the neighborhood. I used to go to her house just to get away from the dysfunction in mine.

While growing up, we did not go to church much. We went on holidays, like Easter and Christmas, when they had children's programs. As far as me knowing who God was, He remained a mystery to me. My friend invited me to go to church a couple of times. Little did I know my time in the presence of God as a young lady would be the vessel used to work my way through all the hurt and pain as I maneuvered through this thing called "LIFE." It was only by His grace and mercy that I was unsuccessful with my desire and actual attempts to commit suicide.

As I approached my teen years and entered high school, it seemed like no matter where I went, girls bullied me. I was bullied every time I went outside. This one girl beat me up daily, causing me to run home, crying and refusing to go back outside. When my grandmother got tired of me running away from the fight, she would whoop me each time I ran into the house until I chose to go back outside and fight back. Well, I finally got tired of being beaten on the street and at home, so I fought back. That first fight led to me using that energy to release all the anger, frustration, and hurt I was dealing with. As a result, when someone said something wrong to me or I felt threatened, I would take matters into my own hands. I also had no reverence for authority, so I ended up getting into trouble and was sent to the juvenile detention center for assaulting a girl at school.

When I was released, I didn't know what to do with myself, so I turned to doing something else to try and rid myself of the pain, abuse, and hurt. As a way to gain the love and attention I never received as a child, I began to try finding love from boys—like the kind I received from my brother. When a boy told me he loved me, I believed that if they said it, then having sex with them was the way to seal that love. I was wrong. I always found myself by myself.

I remember when I was 16 years old, I told my grandmother I wanted a baby. "No, you don't," she said. I didn't listen and ended up pregnant. At the age of 17, I gave birth but was still out of control while trying to mask the hurt and pain. I tried finding my way through life with no real understanding of what and why I continued going through so much heartache. Nonetheless, I had to find a way to raise my child as an uneducated and broken young woman…a mother.

Somewhere along the way, I became addicted to drugs and sex. At first, I had sex with men, and when they were not enough to satisfy my insatiable needs, I engaged in same-sex relationships, too. I thought I was finding my way and making a living because, again, to me, that was "love."

## Shade No More Pain: Released and Set Free

When I grew tired of living my life the way that I was, I found myself searching for this "Jesus" I had heard of since my youth. Little by little, I gave Him a try. In finding Him, I can truly say that all I went through has taught and is still teaching me that my purpose is bigger than me. As I reflect on all I endured in my life, I know that God's plans for me are much greater than the ones I had for myself. Today, I am free from the things that tried to make me feel abandoned. Today, I realize those seeds were only there to try and kill my destiny. The whole time, God was with me, which is why I can testify that when the Son sets you free, you are free indeed (John 8:36)!

**Reflection Question:**

What about your past has left you feeling abandoned, rejected, hurt, or alone? How have you overcome your trials and tribulations?

_____
_____
_____
_____
_____
_____
_____
_____
_____
_____
_____
_____
_____
_____
_____
_____
_____
_____

Shade No More Pain: Released and Set Free

# Tosha Dearbone
## It Stops Here

As you go on this journey with me, I hope that you will pause to assess the relationships in your life.

For me, it all started as a self-evaluation and the continued thoughts of why I battled with emotional unstableness. What is it that many will say? *"Emotional unstableness is what they call a* 'Borderline Personality Disorder' *— better known as a mental illness characterized by a long-term pattern of unstable relationships, distorted sense of self, and strong emotional reactions."*

In 2018, I was told by a therapist that what I thought was "depression" was actually not. Rather, it was an "emotional disorder." As she spoke, I sat quietly, trying to focus on why she would say that about me. Was it truly something I dealt with internally that caused me to have crying spells, thoughts of suicide, and feelings of being unworthy or unloved?

I started to tune in to what I was telling her, listening as I spoke my own words, and wondered: **What made her conclude I was contending with an emotional disorder?!**

When she asked questions about my relationships with my mother, father, and siblings, I began by responding about my dad. He passed away when I was seven years old, so I honestly had no relationship with him while growing up. All I can seem to recall about him was the tragedy that took place on my last visit to his apartment: I was sexually abused by my cousin when my dad went to the store. Being that I was only seven at the time (and afraid), I thought about what would happen if I told my dad. Instantly, the same question flooded my thoughts: *"Do I tell? Do I tell? Do I tell?"* I didn't want **anything** to happen to my dad on account of me. The fear of him being harmed or going to jail scared me, so I kept quiet about the molestation.

I then shared with the therapist about my relationships with my brothers and how I felt as if I didn't fit in. Yes, you read that correctly. I thought I **had** to fit in with my male counterparts in the home because I was made to feel like the outcast. Why? I don't know. Maybe it was a learned behavior. I was always talked about and criticized because I had children at an early age and walked the 'Single Motherhood Walk.' The name-calling was incessant, too! There's one statement that stood out the most: *"Nobody is going to want you with four kids!"* I was left to feel as if that was my truth. I truly believed my brothers' words and actions showed they didn't love or care about me. Crazy, I know.

Then, the therapist asked about my relationships with my children. I told her we were good but also shared how my oldest daughter expressed how she "did not like me" when she was growing up. That saddened me, to the point that I just wanted to give up on parenting her. I was clueless as to what her "assessment" of me was based upon. Allow me a moment to reflect on my life at the time:

- I was 16 years old when I gave birth to her.
- Her father and I were on good terms…until I found out he was cheating on me. (I **instantly** became outraged because I just couldn't believe he would do me like that.)
- As the years passed and child support was set in place, he began to make my daughter uncomfortable by telling her, "Your mother needs to drop the case."
  - **NOTE:** Constantly listening to someone's negative thoughts may cause you to view someone else as the enemy.

I feel like him saying that sent my daughter on a type of rampage against me, as she didn't understand why I wouldn't concede to his demand. I remember telling her often, "I won't drop the case because he needs to take care of you." She wasn't hearing it. Then, as she got older, she came up with **another** factor of why she did not like me. She said, *"It was because you didn't hug me and show affection."* Wow! That set me back…

At that moment, I returned to that seven-year-old little girl who was touched on and made to do things with my little hands. I believed being affectionate was associated with someone doing inappropriate things with and to me. As a result, I was afraid to show her and my other children motherly love. (The enemy sure is cunning, isn't he?) It didn't help that I could not share with them what had been done to me. I didn't want to confuse their innocent, little minds.

However, it didn't stop there!

When the therapist and I began to talk about the relationship with my mom, I immediately started to cry. I felt as if I had just been hit with a bat over and over, and my body began to tremble. Just hearing *anything* about my mom frustrated me and made me very emotional.

**Therapist:** *"So, tell me: How was your relationship with your mom growing up?"*

**Me:** *"Well, it was okay, but not close."*

**Therapist:** *"What do you mean when you say, 'Not close'?"*

**Me:** *"Well, we didn't do mother/daughter things, such as have conversations about the things I liked, school, boys, friends, and stuff moms typically ask their daughter out of curiosity to learn more. I was truly seeking answers from her about my background."*

**Therapist:** *"So, tell me: What **did** you and she do together?"*

**Me:** *"We went shopping on the weekends and maybe out to eat. That's really it."*

**Therapist:** *"How did that make you feel?"*

**Me:** *"It made me feel like she was more of a homegirl rather than my mom. It made me feel alone and rejected because she could hold conversations with my brothers about anything. Not to mention, she constantly bragged about their girlfriends and how much she loved them. As for me, I would often get this "stank" look – as if I disgusted her. For many years, the lack of a relationship with my mom took a toll on me. I would mask it down with a smile, stay out of her way, and try to make myself invisible as much as I could. That sent me on a journey of feeling depressed, like I was a nobody, continuous crying spells, and suicide attempts. I thought, "Maybe if I were dead, she would finally be satisfied with me." All I ever wanted was my momma to see me as her daughter and tell me she loved me without it sounding fake or pressured."*

**Therapist:** *"I am sorry you are feeling this way, but I want you to know it's not depression you are battling. Instead, you are dealing with an **emotional disorder**."*

**Me:** *Staring at her like **SHE** needed to be the one 'on the couch.'*

**Therapist:** *"Can you recall what happens when you begin to feel sad, suicidal, or unwanted?"*

**Me:** *"When my mom and I get into an argument. The same applies to my daughter."*

**Therapist:** *"Those are your triggers."*

For just one moment, can you imagine knowing your **mother** and **daughter** are the triggers that leave you feeling unworthy, inadequate, shunned, or the cause of hurt?

That day in therapy, I cried so much. I just *knew* God was going to punish me for speaking up about how I truly felt. However, I never imagined speaking up was just what I needed to release the soul ties of emotional unstableness. After my confession and from that day forward, I began to examine my thoughts by asking myself, *"How does **this** make me feel?"* If for one *millisecond*, I thought it was too much at that moment, I would cower, as if someone were swinging a balled-up fist at me.

I had to figure out how to conquer those emotions! I began to seek God, listened to sermons about soul ties and toxic behaviors, and stopped ducking and running every time life was difficult. I also set boundaries and learned the value of forgiveness. I wouldn't say I sought or expected an apology from my momma. Rather, forgiveness was moreso for me. I had to forgive her the same way Jesus forgave me (and you) as He got up on that cross.

*"Then said Jesus, 'Father, forgive them, for they know not what they do.'"* (Luke 23:34)

Through the process, I found the strength to express myself with words, not anger or fear of conflict. I had to say it exactly how I heard it, without (of course) sounding as if I am condemning others in any way. I knew deep in my heart that many people could not take constructive criticism without getting upset.

One day, I listened to a sermon by my pastor that said something about, *"You have to see the person or thing as the enemy in order to break free."* That message immediately spoke directly to my spirit-woman. I then took to Facebook in a private group where I shared a message of how I had to see my momma as the enemy in order to break generational curses, release toxic behaviors, and to find my true identity. The seed was planted long before I was born, but it was now up to me to stop the cycle. I had to decide — once and for all — that I would no longer be defeated. I vowed to have a healthy relationship with **my** daughter. After all, I owed her that. She was *never* the enemy, but rather a victim of the crossfire of my emotional bondage. Today, she and I have a much better understanding, and she knows I love her with my whole heart.

As for my mom and me, there are still some challenging days, but I know with God's help, it's all coming full circle. I am her only daughter, and she is my only mother. God gave me to her for a purpose, and I believe without a shadow of a doubt that it was to show her that even through her darkness, she could birth someone who can assist her in her own emotional pain and torment. **I was birthed for a time like this.** My mother's identity **will** be found, and she **will** know her worth. *I am not the enemy.*

Being a survivor of many things — sexual abuse, physical abuse, verbal abuse, teen pregnancy, and abandonment — didn't start with me. My mother was victimized as well. I am decreeing and declaring today:

# IT STOPS HERE!

Rejection doesn't live here anymore. Neither does jealousy, confusion, or false evidence appearing real. If it never registered with you before, I pray you hear me now:

## I FORGIVE YOU.

*"Then He [Jesus] said to me, 'My grace is sufficient for you, for My strength is made perfect in weakness.' Therefore, most gladly, I will rather boast in my infirmities, that the power of Christ may rest upon me."* (2 Corinthians 12:9)

As I end this journey, I leave you with these words of wisdom: **FORGIVE.** Forgiveness is for you. Do not carry the weight of excess luggage that will keep you bound. Instead, share your truth so that you can be healed as you unpack and release. The lighter the load, the better your journey will be.

Following is the declaration I spoke over myself in order to truly be free. You are welcome to speak it over your life as well.

*Lord, I decree and declare that I live for Your approval alone. Help me to need only Your approval. I will not conform to the ways of the world or change who You called me to be to please people. Help me to believe and know that You love me just the way I am. I believe You have healed my brokenness. The spirit of rejection shall have no power of me. Your name is my strong tower. I run into it, and I am safe.*

**~ Proverbs 18:10 ~**

**Reflection Question:**

Looking back over your life, would you say that rejection played a role? If so, how embedded was it, and how did you overcome? If not rejection, what was the prominent factor that shaped who you are today?

_____

_____

_____

_____

_____

_____

_____

_____

_____

_____

_____

_____

_____

_____

_____

_____

_____

_____

_____

# Conclusion

Who would have thought we would have to endure so much pain to reach the other side? So much has been divulged in this book, including instances of:

- Sexual abuse
- Absent parent
- Rejection
- Suicide attempts
- Teenage dating violence
- Domestic violence
- Verbal abuse
- Teen pregnancy
- People-pleasing
- Low self-esteem
- Identity crisis
- And so much more.

Destiny now awaits us all—writer and reader alike. Starting today, walk with your heads held high, knowing that our God is Love. We have waited until our seasoned years to go back and get who we used to be, but that's okay because there was no time limit. God just wanted to see to it that our life experiences — whether good or bad — help someone else.

In closing, I would like to thank each contributor for sharing her story. Without a doubt, I know that each testimony left an impact on someone's heart. Your truths made it a little easier for the next woman to begin her **AUTHENTIC** healing process.

I know it probably wasn't easy to revisit those dark places, those old thoughts, or maybe even those secrets that your elders or other family members told you to keep — those "What goes on in this house, stays in this house" secrets you never told anyone...until now. I, for one, applaud you for having the courage to use your voice through the writing and sharing of your story with others.

Just like the title says, *Shade No More Pain: Released and Set Free*, we are just that! **RELEASED! SET FREE!** No more silence. No more hiding. No more pain. As women of great destiny, we can now say we are fulfilling that critical, God-ordained part of our journey!

## Meet the Authors
*(in order of appearance)*

*Compiler*

Tosha Dearbone

Tosha R. Dearbone

*Foreword By:*

*Latoya Christman*

Shade No More Pain: Released and Set Free

## Contributing Author

## Arthenius Jackson

Tosha R. Dearbone

*Contributing Author*

*Desirae Jefferson*

## Contributing Author

## Francesca Thomas

Tosha R. Dearbone

*Contributing Author*

*Johnetta Bennett*

## Contributing Author

# Keinosha Keaton

Tosha R. Dearbone

*Contributing Author*

La'Toya Spann

## Contributing Author

## Shalita McKnight

Tosha R. Dearbone

*Contributing Author*

Sherra Byrd

## Contributing Author

## Shglenda Green

Tosha R. Dearbone